Lift

Lift

POEMS BY Luray Gross

 RAGGED SKY PRESS
PRINCETON, NEW JERSEY

Published by Ragged Sky Press
270 Griggs Drive, Princeton, NJ 08540
www.raggedsky.com

Cover art © 2018 Janet Wormser, *Rhapsody*, 2012, oil on linen, 24" x 20"
Book and cover design: Jean Foos
All Rights Reserved
ISBN 978-1-933974-31-6
Library of Congress Control Number: 2018958171

This book has been composed in Fairfield, FF Scala and Neue Haas Unica Pro
Printed on acid-free paper ∞
Printed in the United States of America

for David Keller and Peter Wood

mentors, friends

Contents

IV. The Place Beyond Language

V. Thirst

Epilogue

Prologue

Lift

Day breaks. You want to snap that string
of mistakes that's tied you to the past.
You've been reading your fortunes
upside down, jumbling the words
and lucky numbers until they're a maze.

But now, for no apparent reason,
your arches flex, your toes push off
in easeful synchrony.

At the end of Ogden Street,
you reach the tracks
and find a gravel crossing—shortcut
to Lemon Hill and the river beyond.

If you were a little wooden boat,
you would be floating on that mirror of light,
sails set, cargo balanced.

A startle of doves whistles to sky
winging in all directions—
every one of them, home.

I
Fodder

What I Do

I ask life to give me more fodder,
more tough stuff to pass through the shredder.
Then it happens—the rope, the crash,
slice, bruise, clash, the anomalous cell.
Sometimes just a dream that tastes like sour milk.

This morning, a room full of dismissive third graders
with a teacher focused on math. Nothing I do
or do not do gathers them
into a world beyond quantification.
What's it worth? their shoulders ask.
Their chairs rasp across the floor.

Happiness, some say, can be sought and found
or found if one gives up seeking. Lately,
I've adopted a stray notion that keeps trotting
just a shadow's length behind my heels, quiet
with no collar and tags to jingle, no yip or growl.
Perhaps I will name it Heart's Desire, Beloved,
Gem of the Night. If it answers, will it stay?

Saved

It's easy being saved, once you get the knack.
It happens without your really having to do a thing.
That avalanche in Russia, the incendiary device
strapped beneath a zealot's shirt: you've done
absolutely nothing to survive either one,
yet here you are scrubbing potatoes
and admiring the broccoli's bodybuilder arms.

You failed to get vaccinations for either kind of flu
and just yesterday ordered from a grimy menu
and neglected to wash your hands
before gripping that turkey sandwich,
but you feel not one jot worse
than you did the day before.

Being saved, it turns out,
is like waking in the morning
with a sweet dream still playing
on the big screen behind your eyelids.

Why leave being saved to somebody's god
or the state's idea of justice,
when mercy pours from one cupped hand
into the other like a Slinky fresh from the box?

You will travel far and wide, both pleasure and business.
Who cares whether the fortune does
or does not turn out to be true?

You don't need to explain what you did not earn:
the melting sheets of lake ice that sang to you
as the breeze rocked them, the perfect feather
that fell at your feet, the fist that unclenched,
then reached for your reluctant hand.

Even the fearing door,
the one you pass again and again,
keeps on opening into light.

Snake Lifts Its Body

Snake lifts its body
with no arms to push off,
no hands to press.

Harder, my father insisted,
lean into the muscles and press—

Father melancholy, mother mischief,
sister shadow, sister wound, sister wit.

Language broken
to bit and bridle,
saddle and command,
rein against the neck.

What do I want and why do I want it?
I want to want and sometimes I do.

Cedars fern the afternoon sky
nearly too distant to bear
even in the mind.

If I had a word for it once
I've forgotten it now. *fading memories*

You Think You're Not Ready to Write Poetry

You are wrong.
Your cat may be throwing up on the counterpane.
Your refrigerator may just have died. You may
be leaving for an interview in five minutes, and
your old boyfriend may be at the door with posies
and an apology. You may be eating ice cream
or crème brûlée; you may be booking flights
to Houston or LA. You may have no fears,
no troubles, no loves or ecstasy,
but you are prepared for poetry:
you were lifted from a cut in your mother's belly
or made your way through the close of the birth canal.
You took your first gulp of dangerous air.
Some part of you remembers,
though it isn't your brain.
You opened your mouth. You wailed
or perhaps the wail still pushes against your sternum, stifled.
You were wrapped in sterile linens or laid
on a rough blanket, set down in grasses and leaves.
You learned the nipple, the pull and swallow.
This was just the beginning, just
the first hours of your history. What more do you need?
You have studied encyclopedias written by wind
and by water. You have shopped in the mall of false desire
and paid with your sweat. You have thirsted, you have envied,
you have dreaded and denied.
What's your excuse?
Malaise, distraction, repression?
Which of the antique vices would you claim?
You say you have no words, explaining with words.
Listen: in your dreams, a world blossoms,
whole phrases rise and float
ready to be heard.

What Would Spinoza Think?

"What would Spinoza think?" I thought
as stiltgrass succumbed to my tugging,
and roots of curly dock held.
Long ago he'd been a partner to my thoughts.
This morning I would not have recognized him
had he been kneeling next to the lima beans.

How does one keep alive the life of the mind?
At lunch I consult the old encyclopedia:
spinning jenny, spinning wheel, spire
on the same two-page spread as Baruch Spinoza,
Dutch philosopher, who chose to grind lenses
rather than accept Louis XIV as patron,
turned down a position at a German university as well.

Thrown out of the synagogue at twenty-four for his ideas
and for admitting them, did he grab the collars of the faithful
trying to convince them that only with their rational minds
could they be free? What would he say
about these hours spent weeding vegetables,
hoisting hay, brushing loose hair from the dog?

Baruch, I was born to the work of the body,
raised carrying buckets and bales, fetching cows
and tending infants, ironing, scrubbing,
stitching, steaming, chopping, stirring.
When words and ideas falter, I trust my hands.

You turned yours to the art of
scattering and gathering light,
knowing surely a lens rightly held
will set tinder to smolder,
and breath, carefully directed,
turn that smolder
to flame.

Song of Ignorance, Song of Bliss

I love numbers for their profiles
and their tendency to dance.
The way round-bellied 5 leans into
slope-shouldered 6.

I love the engines of equations,
the plus and times and greater/lesser than.
Carve them on my gravestone
and let the wind puzzle them out.

I read the dictionary with my blind thumb—
thump, thumpety-thump
diagonally down the page.

Each morning I skim the papers.
Even the headlines I forget by dusk.
How did that one laugh? How small
were his reaching hands?

The boxcars carried their hungry freight,
chugging along the terrible tracks to Treblinka,
Auschwitz. Most who saw, most who heard
are dead, but are they as dead
as those who crowded cold in the dark?

The kingfisher rattles back and forth.
All winter long he patrolled the muddy creek
believing, it seemed, in singing,
like a ten-year-old unaware of his monotone.

There's always a song
before the end of the world.
A little song of ignorance, a song of bliss

like the songs I try to cultivate,
melodies rich in rests
for all of us sated with talk.

We sing a little song for the living, for the dead.
A song for the wrists of the hostage, for the row of corpses.
A song for the bullet, innocent
as any stone.

Fox Follows

I

Under the long moon, fox calls and calls
not to me or anyone else in this house;
but we waken, trying to translate that want,
that need, that possible joy.

In the morning, our dogs pull
toward the musk. They read news
of which I remain ignorant
even though I taste it in the air.

At noon, fox lolls in the sun,
rises and trots, pausing now and then
to look my way.

II

In the field, at the slaughterhouse,
the meal begins.
In piss and shit, it ends.

What life does not deserve memory and regard?

III

Fox follows, catches up at every corner.
He leans against a post and leers
through his mask of red and white papier-mâché.

I change my body for that of a man
covered in swirled inscriptions,
but fox is not fooled, does not quit.

I cross the river, I lie in wait.
I take up oriental discipline.
Fox ambles toward me.

IV

He has taken off his mask.
He carries it through the brown grasses.

I crouch, I spring,
I grab fox by the throat, shake and shake,
and then let go.

I churn in my bed like a shell in the surf.
Fox shivers away like rain.

Epistemology I

Before the concert, the oboe player
slipped off one red pump
and slid it back on. Then
her breath filled the space
with plaintive sound.

She sat right in front of us—
close, yet distant
as the deer that make their way
up from the valley while we sleep,
their hooves denting the mossy lawn.

And the one that leapt across River Road
scarcely touching the right fender
before disappearing into a field—
maimed or not, I'll never know.

Nor will I know, most likely,
just what brushed against my hand
as it flew into dusk, its flight
the slightest whirr.

I imagine it a perky house wren,
familiar with us from walks
past the wood's edge where it forages,
chattering and wagging its saucy tail.

How many evenings
does it nestle in the clothespin bag
hanging at the corner of the shed?

This is the world I want,
felt as much as seen or heard.
Nearly held, nearly known.
This world,
not the implausible next.

II

House with No Keys

House with No Keys

We never locked our doors.
Ghosts would still have found the keyhole,

and this way we felt prepared, even for
Dad's great uncle Peter, the shotgun powder

black against his cheek. We'd nod, offer him a chair.
Any night, the mute with a trunkful

of gadgets for sale might walk in and join us;
we always suspected he was hungry for company,

but just too proud. We did not expect the bear.
Not one of us had dreamed his dense fur

or his keen black snuffling.
The afternoon the bear arrived seemed

ordinary, warm enough to melt the butter in the butter plate.
Our dog lay motionless on the cool basement floor.

As I stood in the kitchen with the freezer open,
enjoying the chill that tumbled out,

waiting for our mother to make me close it,
the back door opened. There was a delicate manner

about its walk across the red linoleum
on into the dining room, right past the table

and out the front door. Sometimes when I enter a room,
I too might as well be a draft or a snatch of music from a passing car.

A woman smiles and nods, but not for me.
Not in the least offended, I stretch my claws.

By the time we picked up the phone, the bear was gone.
We've never stopped telling the story.

Our Father's Hands

Torches appeared at the tips of his fingers.
Two by two, he tossed them at the bears
who rumbled like waves out of the dark.

We perched on the grape arbor
where he'd put us
like fledglings told not to fly.

I hold the dream in the corner of my mouth
like a smooth pink pebble, taking it out
now and then to shine before it dulls.

Against those claws, those shoulders,
the dense stench of their fur,
our father threw fire.

Light leapt from his hands, arced
across the frozen lawn. He kept the bears
at bay while behind us, the huge house
reared back on our history.

If Two People Are Aware of the Rising Moon

When his mind grew empty
and his heartbeat slowed to a vague stutter,
our father no longer walked his fields at night.

He did not call to say, "Look at the moon. You have to see it."
Even grown, even when his authority rankled,
we had obeyed.

Mind empty, he lost hold
of hurts he had suffered, the unrequited loves.
Shame that had festered seemed to heal.

We could not follow him to that country
of no nationality, no creed. None of us but
his granddaughter, who had gone before,

though sometimes we nearly met him there
in a vast silence that covered the world's persistent hum.
His melancholy had prepared the place

since those blue boyhood afternoons
he stood on the back porch,
borrowed violin tucked under his chin,
bow scraping the open strings.

A Walk with the Future Pastor Johnson

"May I touch your breasts?" His question was
civil as a shoe salesman's offer of assistance.
There seemed no reason to say no,
even though, or perhaps because,

the question came from a boy
who had been in my Sunday School class
since long before either of us had gotten glasses
or made the Honor Roll.

We'd strayed from the group
at the Luther League retreat
and ended up on a grassy slope,
sitting side by side engaged, at first,

in a vaguely theological discussion
full of questions without definite answers.
"Yes," I said, then sat still
while he lifted my sleeveless blouse and

slipped his fingers inside the cotton cups of my bra.
How unhurried were his explorations
of this strange world, round with plenty.
How tender were the ministrations of his hands.

I kept my gaze on the narrow road
that curved and disappeared among the trees,
then reappeared thin and gray
before disappearing once again.

No matter where it led,
some day I'd take a road like that.

What Took Me There

Was it Dr. Richardson's shock of white hair
or the assignments he gave in Philosophy 101?
Was it Barbara Dixon's wan worldly smile?
Was it dancing drunk in navy tights and that short
orange jumper? Was it singing each Sunday
in the college chapel choir?

Vultures circled high, then low,
over the mound of rock and earth.
I could not have asked for a better sign.
They read the updrafts for promise of decay

and I stared across that sloping ground
hallowed by death—the famous deaths
of civil war, the daily deaths of cells—
and decided I would live
even if this world was all there was.

My friend waited in his car, smoking
a thin French cigarette. Kindly
he had brought me there, and
kindly he would take me back.

Listening to Edith Piaf at Nineteen

"Je ne regrette rien," she sang.
Rien: the word filled as a vein fills
when the tourniquet is untied.

Nothing became *something* so completely
it was acceptable again to have a body.
Unhappy, but still incarnate.

The catechist poses questions
just to answer them. I thought I was done
with argument, but I was simply beginning,
using the clay I'd been molding since my first cry.
Knowing/not knowing drifted through the smoky room.

The "r" rolled up from my throat,
the "n" barely escaping my ribs.
Between them, the vowels,
light enough to float, yet held.

Nothing, I needed nothing other
than what I already had,
that tensile thread of sound.

Apology

I abandoned the small boat.
Moored, unmoored—
I could not know.

No star shone.
Rocks battered
the pulsing strait.

I knocked at a keep of bone,
heartwood solid.
I knocked, I knocked
against the fierce-barred door.

Air was waiting, and
I would have it.
Mother,
I did not mean you harm.

Reliquary

Removed from its white glove of stillness,
the hand wants to touch
every single thing—*feather, blood, bone.*

More intimate than the eye—
wind, word, phantom limb.

The hand wings, black, into sky.

An apple falls roundly, repeatedly,
an Escher elaboration of apple.
The hand accepts and gives away.

No rest for the hand
once sprung from the womb.

No. Even there my hands were busy
reading currents, writing messages
only the blind could hope to decipher.

The blind, the disappeared, the ones
who no longer are.
You, Mother, among them.

A Small Thing to Ask

The faithful remember Jerusalem every day,
but Mother, I seem to forget you
for weeks at a time, though you keep smiling

from the little photograph on our refrigerator,
with the yellow-suited infant tucked
in the crook of your right arm. Nothing,
it seems, is bothering either of you.

I walk past every day barely noting,
but tonight your glance caught me, urging
Call, call me, and some slight

obedient part of my brain
that doesn't mark years or losses or gains
inclined toward the phone

to hear your voice, that brief
pause before *Hello.* Perhaps a diminutive
added to my name, a hint of a joke without malice.

It seemed such a small thing to ask,
like blood from a turnip, like a sea without salt,
like sight restored: an angel stirring the waters
so that someone, some lucky someone
might be healed.

Mother, Still Gone

She appeared and spoke,
but not to me. She returned,
and I only happened to be there,
an accidental witness to her sly approach.

I could tell she held a private joke
close to her chest, close to the scar
and the one small breast near the place
we were all once told the heart was hidden.

Was she dressed in yellow? In spring green?
The dream did not reveal.
It could have been an episode
in black and white,
though her image did not flicker,
just recede.

In the field across the road,
three stout crows took their ease.
Clouds gathered,
the weight of sky assembling itself.
Darts of sleet closed the afternoon.
I could not help but feel
her indifference everywhere.

Fibonacci Reverie

Familiar emptiness.

Then the apparition
of a glass half empty,
another half full. Both
swept to the floor.

Three cards in the hand,
five under the table.
In the sober church on the hill,
a double string quartet, eight bows sawing away.

Thirteen donuts, cookies, ears of corn—
whatever the person behind the counter, baker or not,
decides to drop into the bag.

Under the basket, who's first to reach twenty-one?

Thirty-four and pregnant, I lie on the floor
and gather our cranky firstborn into my arms,
settle her on my chest and belly. We sleep
while the child still hidden kicks and tumbles.

Fifty-five bottles of beer on the wall, fifty-five bottles of beer
my mother, who likely never sipped from even one,
sang as she steered the station wagon with one hand,
wagged the fingers of the other to the broken-record tune.

I suppose I could keep the sequence going,
counting and naming, naming and counting
geese lifting from the field, cars before me at the tollbooth,
bubbles before they break.

This morning, a single jet arrowed west toward clear blue,
away from the ranks of gray-pink clouds, through which the one sun

began to rise. Clouds too many to count, I took the time to think,
thinking too of calendar photos—Arizona canyons lit by slanting sun,
one beyond the other, more and more
beyond the camera's reach,

an intimation of endlessness lent to the child
who turned the page from August to September,
the month of her birth, the month of school and its rupture.

There would be no escaping the vast and hungry future.

When You Walk

beginning with a line from William Stafford

Things come toward you when you walk.
The poplar that stood in one place
for a hundred years draws closer,
even though the horizon keeps falling away.

When you walk, the wood pigeon's murmur
and the magpie's racket
deliver themselves to your ears.
You don't have to try.

The child with her back turned,
scuffing one foot over the other, turns.
You know her, as though a mirror
were held before your face,
and for once the image is true.

When you walk, the wagon is stacked high
with fragrant hay. Your father stands waiting.
You walk toward him and try to push pity
from your mind. No, he is coming toward you
to make amends.

Out

I

I wanted out, not in
to any other there
or when. Wanted that slap
of the screen door
to be the final punctuation mark.

Wanted to keep walking
and let nowhere
take me,
wanted to shrink, wrapping
myself tight.

I wanted out
of that hour, away
from the nothing
of your blank face.
Nothing admitted,
nothing asked.

I wanted the chamber
to eject me, a mouth
to spit me out.

I wanted passage
with no reckoning,

no points fixed,
no root to the square.

I was done with calculation
and finding the mean.

II

Among the reeds
blackbirds asserted
their claims.

Dark was falling
but I was holding on,
of two minds.

Wanting
the wild, wanting
to become
untamed, untethered

but wanting more—
it must be true—

to have been sought
and, finally, found.

Liminal

for Paul

Sharp-edged cumuli
sailed north
as we flew south. I could not
see them as anything
but solid, impenetrable,
imperturbable.

There are days when I'm edgy.
I'm aiming to jump.
I'm simmer and seethe,
roiling toward rock.

It's then
you corral me.
You dial back the heat.
Show me edge is not end.
It's reprieve.

Curriculum Vitae

I come from a womb that came from a womb
where one child thrived and one child failed.

Some days I am nothing but bluster. Bluster, and this
small dance I let my hips lean into before they snap back.

When I was eight I starved my pet rabbits.
I slapped my sisters and mastered the art of the pout.

I spent junior high in the fiction section
and cautiously befriended the halt and the lame.

Now the worm is my mentor, blind and persistent.
The wind is my friend and the dog who does not speak.

I worship the ball bearing
singing, spinning and hidden as it works.

My hands reach from side to side, my breadth,
my height, no adequate measure or reach.

Still, the harmed boy turns out his sadness in the paddock of my arms
then runs and somersaults across the spindly stream.

The brainy girl child with thorny braces grazes in the tiny pasture
of my attention. She tastes the young grass, breathes in its scent.

My man calls me beautiful, though he knows
how it feels to be wounded by words.

Sometimes I pray to the god I scarcely believe in:
Let me be still. Let me be mute and burnished.

III

Singing to the Stone

Aftermath

Leaf, leaf. Sparrow, sparrow.
Morning calm. First day.
Name what the world gives.
Begin with two words at a time.

Fence, fence. Gate, gate. No
and no. Minus and minus again
against which
all our summing is no measure:

the taut skin of his ankles,
arc of the pelvis, the bow of his brow.
His seeping wound.

We add and add
never reaching the one
that until this just-passed,
last-breath silence was.

You were wrong and I was right,
minus proclaims. Obdurate,
we must recite the lesson over and over
as we board the express, as we rinse the spoons,
let them clink in our hands.

We look for the truce,
though another war will come.
We wait for that which grows after the mowing:
another harvest.
Sword blades, grass blades.
The scythe, the sickle hung back in the shed.
The field left to green.

Civil War

How the war had started, none of
us in the schoolyard knew or wondered.
Knowing second graders
passed the game down to the firsts.

We piled rocks among tree roots,
fortified our positions.
We hollered and leapt. We fell,
ecstatic grounded constellations.

Our mothers cinched the belts
of their shirtwaist dresses, drove us
to piano lessons, read Little Golden Books
over and over, each word a promise kept.

Back from their own wars,
our uncles, our fathers, inhaled,
ground out their cigarettes,
never spoke of their wounds.

Catechetical

Blood testifies to the work of the knife
and the captor's hood will silence the eye.
Daylight cautions the dream, though sometimes
dreams hold off the enterprising light.

Does the kernel call back to the silk?
Does the breast bid farewell
to the sweet blue milk?
Does bone hum along with the silver ankle-bells?

I believe the bough calls to the breeze,
just as the cello speaks to the bow.
The cave echoes the hand that etches
its sheltered walls.

What must the piston preach to the spark?
What does the rifle announce
to the shell as it speeds away?

What does a kiss
say to the mouth
that spends and spends?

The Armies

The grief-armies assemble, but I'm not going with them.
—Rumi

The army of the spear, lance, charger, chariot,
and the miniaturized nuclear warhead.
Army of the bayonet, bazooka, mortar, Kalashnikov;
of the tank, machine gun, IED, suicide vest.

They assemble: private armies
and those of the republic.
Domestic-duty armies and those with long-range,
short-range, medium-range missiles.

Army with napalm and mustard gas.
The slingshot, the arrow, the well-sprung bow.
Army of cavalry, infantry, legion, brigade.
Of ambush and advance. The trench. The retreat.

Army of the lie and the half-lie.
Army of tents, of barracks.
Army that moves on its stomach,
that starves and freezes.

Army of the quartermaster, foot soldier,
sergeant, lieutenant, general;
fraught with dysentery, yellow fever,
gangrene, homesickness, malaise.

Such an army, I, being female,
was neither forced nor enticed to join,
and the army none of us can help but join:

the grief-army
with no howitzers,
pistols, poisons, or plots.

The army each of us was born into
with our heart beating its quick-time march.
There, any cove might become a beach-head,
any pallet, a bier.

To the Door

Who can open the door of the green river?   —Zuhur Dixon, Iraq

Today brings more news of bombings,
of beheadings and threats of beheadings.
Why does it seem necessary to mention this
when all I want to do is celebrate the door?

Doors swinging on hinges,
doors held open, admitting air,
and doors revolving in cylinders of glass.
Doors of steel, of wood, of paper, of cloth.

Doors of beads jostling on their strings,
all sliding doors slick in their tracks,
and those little flaps of the heart
opening, closing, opening.

Leaving the apartment, the lovers
remove the steel bar, push back the bolt.
She was a child in a house without locks
but here they insert each key,
listen for the slide and click.

Is it really necessary
to think of the flaps of prison tents,
of cords binding ankles and wrists?

In Iraq the provisional government totters.
Leaflets begging for the life
of a hostage drift to the ground.
How is their Arabic, one wonders.

It is a difficult language, a teacher explains,
demonstrating sounds not common in English:
glottal stops, fricatives and glides. Difficult,
he says, but beautiful.

The door of the mouth opens and closes
and sounds escape: sounds of laughter,
sounds of weeping, urgent
to any tongue.

Triptych: January 2009

I

Aquamarine—not just a word,
but shoulders rising, cresting like some urge.
Afternoon light cathedraled through waves,
the urge itself illuminating
not mind, but body
older than any description of itself,
old as its own voice, its *mama-mama*
Its own *I am.*

II

Shrapnel enters the baby's body
while his mother holds him in her arms.
His head flops back and she knows.
Three days sheltered in this room.
Thirty of her family already dead,
and now this.
In Gaza. Now.

III

Lumeena wears white.
She taps the sides of singing bowls.
Lumeena heals with trances.
When she prays, it does not matter
who listens. Her face is a heart.
Go, she says, *Go.*

The Dead of Shiloh Call Out

The dead of Shiloh call out to the dead of Baghdad,
to the hungry children of Iraq, to the half-blind dog
who barks at grains of salt jangling in the spoon.

Oil burners flame and fume across the nation.
Our president polishes his middle initial
and narrows his gaze. "A long time" shrinks

and shrinks. A short time grows.
Threat and alert become the same word.
In a department store, a young woman

and her full-term belly fall to the floor.
Death pins her beside the merchandise.
Just before his enlightenment,

the seated Buddha touched finger to ground,
calling earth to witness the deeds of his life,
calling forth water to chase away evil.

In the world beyond this world,
the woman strides into the future.
Her loins are a fish trying to swim

in the opposite direction. Her ribs are a grate
for wind to blow through, for the river to enter.
Her breasts are bread. Her collarbones, a crosspiece.

Her eyes scan the urgent sea.
She asks each god just one question.
Forward, forward is the only answer.

Fire under Mountain

The cold moon wanes, the wolf moon waits.
She writes of angels and wears her flesh like snow.
Fire under mountain, the rain falls down.

Swan's wrenched wing like a grudge against God.
My father weeps, the whole room trembles.
Fire under mountain and rain falls down.

Baby teeth and locks of hair, a small brass key.
To hold the river, you must flow.
Fire under mountain, rain falls down.

Mother laughed, and the Bible flew out the window.
We never knew her secret name.
Fire under mountain and rain falls down.

Cat wakes the piano in the middle of the night.
Our children turn in their sleep and sleep on.
Fire under mountain, the rain falls down.

Light conceals its thousand forms.
I memorize the gorgeous names of bones.
Fire under mountain, rain falls down.

The president pardons himself each morning.
His enemies' blood grows thick with iron.
Fire under mountain and rain falls down.

An accident is waiting for its purpose.
Missile idles, knife quivers in its sheath.
Fire under mountain, rain falls down.

Fire smolders. Rain desists.
Without sky, mountain stops growing.
Fire, fire. We all fall down.

Until You Dig Holes

Martha never lived in the wild.

Her pink handgun, Lucy, goes with her to school,
little lamb will not stay at home.

Muscat proposed to his girlfriend Christina.
An angel peered down at them,
evidence of coverage crossing state lines.

A pretty puzzling war, that War of 1812.
What if your picture were taken without permission?

Nasiriyah, where Jessica Lynch was taken captive.
The home of a fish and rice dish
that couldn't taste sweeter.

You may bruise more easily—
the only hint, an indentation or two in the grass.

Researchers have placed increasing emphasis
on non-motor aspects of the disorder.

De-extinction has been proposed.
The snapshot evolved too.

In the distance, a string of barrows gleams like opal,
a bloke with a cross, some lethargic cows.

Until you dig holes, you just don't
know what you've got.

April: What I Learned

Bloodroot pushes its snub leaves up well before the blossom.
The Tree of Love shows best against an indigo sky.

What repels the deer attracts the dog.
I like throwing things away as much as I like holding on.

Clouds move in even when you aren't noticing.
My father has not given up all hope of love.

According to knowing fourth graders, dressing Gothic costs forty dollars.
Charm may not be a weakness. Sugar will not cure bad coffee.

Prosperous children don't chase a ball across a street.
Eating wild salmon will not necessarily make you wild.

Ten years after the massacre, Tutsi and Hutu turned swamp into rice fields.
The cost to the land has not been calculated.

Circling the city does not ensure success; revenge may not be possible.
God lives in the silence, but beckons us to speak.

On Being Asked to Write a Poem

for C. B.

In China, my friend tells me, one never steps
into the shadow of one's teacher, which is to say
even on days most clouded by despair,
one must walk at a seemly distance

keeping space on each side, space before
and after—a complete circle for the moving shadow,
the teacher's searching mind and its wings.

One of my friend's own students told her this,
but she can't vouch for it in the way she is sure
that in Book Seven of the Analects of Confucius,
the sage is quoted: *If I hold up one corner,
and a man cannot come back to me with the other three,
I do not continue the lesson.*

But we have not read Confucius. We come to class,
to your crowded office, leaning *into* your shadow,
barely keeping hold of one corner, perhaps two,
each time expecting a miracle

to make words lie down on paper like refugees
on a dusty floor, like airplanes settling on tarmac,
like newborns put to sleep on their backs
in a row of plastic cribs.

Surely Sisyphus sang to the stone as he pushed it up
the familiar slope, an intimate song, sung first
for that which gave him pleasure, then pain.
It is what you know, what you teach:
Language will not abandon us,
will say what needs to be said, enough
to make the world a burden we can bear.

IV
The Place Beyond Language

Before Gabriel Arrives

And the angel said to her, "Fear not."
—Luke 1:30

She sits on the stoop
        fourteen
    grown child growing
                nearly woman

a delta
        a river splitting   spilling
                        seeping
                            sought
she presses her thighs
        to grainy concrete

    root   tree   flower   bud

            born to be proud and ashamed
                she knows nothing
                        questions fill her mouth

she holds her hand to the sun
            to test its opaqueness
                        she wants   she wants

she wants to know
                        what it is that she wants
not how to get
            or even how to give

her feet
        in their canvas sneakers
                dream   of dark caverns

but her elbows long to
        unbend in the emptiness between
                herself and the stars

she hears her name
              and does not answer

                    what is her name?

only a word
              like string
        a word like
              metal unmolded
                    a slump   of sound
look at the way
        her freckles insist
                    her skin is what counts

her skin   and its tan smoothness

summer is ending   soon will be
        supper and brothers
and spoons   spoons and plates

        there will be bread   there
              will be butter

no one at the table
                    will see her
        no one
                    will ever know

Fifteen

I thought I knew the place
where the body wants not to continue.
I thought I knew despair,
its stubbed out cigarettes, its unwashed hair.
I thought I knew its rain—cold-needled, wind-driven,
unstoppable. I knew that distance
where every familiar face was turned away
and the small things I once loved—
blue-bottle vase, cat's eye, cool stone stoop—
held no solace, had all turned gray.
I'd looked into that well and heard the voice.
I'd come that close.
But she, the girl we always wanted to find
knocking at our door, was the one
who went to the place beyond language,
and nothing kept her from going there.
Oh, she was too capable, too strong,
able to calculate the distance and anchor the rope.
She was the one who pushed the cabinets into place
and, agile, made the climb. She was the one
who told her mother, "I won't be long"
and did not delay. Or perhaps she did,
then had no choice but push off into air.
I am not convinced there is
any place where she has gone,
though sometimes I remind myself—
as many things exist in the dark
as in the light.

The Ellen Meditations

October 29

Not a valley, but a crevasse with no handholds, no places for the toes to grip.
    All those who have gone before have left no sign.

I write, as though writing will make some mark worthy of standing beside the facts.

Is there any meditation now that is not an Ellen meditation?

Wet snow begins at daybreak. My sister reports her dreams:
    I said, "Ellen, let's go up to the farm," and she answered,
    "I can't, Mom. I'm dead. I didn't mean for it to happen."

    I dreamed that she was blind and Elizabeth came.
    "You don't need to see," I told her. "You can touch each other's faces. You can
    sing together."

October 27

Six weeks have passed and the act seems only more absurd, more unbelievable.

The days are coming, says the prophet, the fierce and glorious days of the Lord, when the
    graves will be rent and the souls released.

What was her hope? From what did she seek release?

October 20

When I try to describe her, it is as though I am describing a face without features.
    I am searching for the face hidden behind that beauty, that abundant *yes.*

The work of the writer, according Ciaran Carson, is to "stumble around" in the world of
    language. Stumble in *why, silence, secret, plunge, leap, precipice.*

Something in the dark that could not be quelled or quenched, faced or fended off.

October 18
How many of us are "half in love with easeful death"?

October 9
On the west coast, three thousand miles from home and facing the return.

Just this: there is nothing else in my personal life that I so badly wish had
    not happened.

October 8
The city glows under full sun, warm sun. We wake early, our bodies still on Eastern time
    and make love. All I think of is my sister, how one does not need the desolation of
    time to become haunted, how it can happen in an instant.

October 4
She cannot stop remembering her twirling, and today tells me this as well: "I keep seeing
    her face, how she looked at me."

September 25
Death and the act of self-destruction have been banished from the Celebration of Life.
    Her brothers and sisters sing. Her parents speak to the assembled crowd. Eleven
    hundred have come, the ushers estimate.

September 20
When the hospital staff removes the ventilator, she takes two breaths. Even now, it is not
    easy for her to die.

When our daughter was two weeks old, a weary woman in the ShopRite looked at her
    and said, "Just wait until she's fifteen." For our child, fifteen came and went and
    we all went on.

September 15
At the hospital, the believers are still praying, still singing.

I am not the only one who knows there will be no miracle.

September 13
She told her mother she was going out to the barn to look for the kittens.

She pushed the cabinet into place and fetched the ladder and climbed and tied the lead of
the yellow halter to the beam, placed the loop around her neck
and stepped into the air.

* * *

January 20
"Four months," my sister says, "four months since Ellen died."

One thing I do not tell her:

There are days I wake in meager light
and open the private book of my heart
to find written there in indelible ink
one word: *Joy.*

The Plain Bread

No god, no human, I think, planned for it to happen.
Not even the girl herself, scaling that height,
arranging the noose and stepping off.
None of us imagined, none of us divined that possibility.
None of us knows how to rightly continue without her
even though we get up each morning.
We chew and swallow.

Year Two

Her parents lose her over and over again.
Each morning they tell themselves, she is dead,
she is still dead.

Another autumn's golds—mottled, molded, marred—
come twirling down. Another story that has no shape
but the shape of falling.

Her mother cuts off the syllables of her own name,
casts the letters aside to wander
like bees that have forgotten the hive.

She is shedding this life
like a garment that never properly fit.
Perhaps it will fall at her feet
and she will not need to notice.

Her father is a boat without a bottom
that spins and spins but refuses to sink.
The mast has no rigging, only a flag
tattered, flapping in the wind.
The country rages. Wild birds lament.

This has all been said a thousand times—
we love only the particular,
those hands, that slim neck, those shoulders,
her boxes of beads, her many-colored scarves.

In a dream, Doctor Death hands me a paper grocery bag
heavy with possible cures. You can try this,
he says, and turns to leave with no further explanation.

Wait, I call out, but he is gone.

Her Death

You wear her death like night on a windowsill,
like dust on the wings of a moth.
You wear it like oil anointing a baby's brow,
like salt in a cut.

You pull it over your head
like a communion dress; you push
each button through its hole. Sometimes
you choose it; sometimes it comes unbidden.

Either way, you feel it against your body,
chill as a glowstick's chemical light.
There are days you think you have slipped
from its grasp. You are wrong.

We poured her ashes into the earth.
Should have poured water, should have poured wine.

The Breezes

Now the breezes talk in the cherry,
brush past the arborvitae,
reach lilac and plum

like hands folding sheets
cool and soft from the line,
edges joined, wrinkles smoothed,

like hands working an old scar
with knowledge of having healed.

I've told you more than once
that's the life I'd choose,

though perhaps I will be reconciled
and let my body bend
to the only life I know.

V
Thirst

After a Death

Remember to breathe—deeply
first out, pressing your palms
toward the earth, the floor that holds you,
then in. Bell your diaphragm, fill your lungs.
Repeat, repeat, repeat.

Place two fingers lightly
over your pulse, that message
your heart keeps sending you.
The carotid above your clavicle will do;
but if you can, lie down, stretch
and find the thump in your groin.

Make love until you exhaust both yourself
and your lover, but do not speak.
Let sweat and cum rime your skin.
Sleep. Do not attempt to
remember your dreams.
Let your waking be slow.
Let water scald the night away.

Eat oranges and salty bread,
tart yogurt and blackberry jam.
Crack an egg into a buttered iron pan
and gently shake until the white
no longer shivers. Turn once
and count to ten before
you slide the egg onto the plate.

Pepper, pepper. Perhaps some salt.
Drink hot coffee, tea if you must.
Live as if each gesture matters.

Dream Variation

I ask the pharmacist
to cut off my ear.
A simple request

unlike that of
the man in front of me
who begs for a refill
before it is due.

Black tongues
lick his forearms,
crawl over his elbows.
He leans close as

she patiently refuses.
Patient as well, I wait
for her to usher me
into the treatment room.

I have been convincing:
an efficient clean cut.
It barely bleeds.

Cutting

She inscribes her belly,
her thigh. Flesh
that clothing will cover.
She tells me this
in a voice dull as a tabletop.

Her pain takes her
beyond the reach
of craft or cunning
to an Erewhon of misery.
Anti-paradise.

In an old illustration,
two angels
cross fiery swords, preventing return
to Eden.

She takes up the blade
in the secret
time and space of her room

to feel—
she says—to feel any
thing

and call it
good.

The Woman Who Loved Winter

loved the shapes of things
and that which shaped them—
skeletons stripped of skin and muscle,
the thrust of frost-heaved sod and hoarfrost
spikes coating a wooden sill.

She loved the wrap and fold of wool,
how her own heat could be conserved.
She loved turning her face to the wind
and quickening her steps.

That wind singing in the wires,
some called it keening.
Some called it song.

She was ever on the lookout for corpses:
the ordinariness of a squirrel
smeared on the road,
the garter snake rune pressed into asphalt.

She needed no books or testimonies
to tell her of the calm
that comes after last breath.

She knew that one day,
when she was truly bereft,
she would come into her own.

In the gallery, she stopped
in front of a print called "Silence,"
a face made, not born.
Nine uneven stitches tugged the lips together.

More accurate, she thought, than any mirror.
Three-quarter moons closed the eyes,
her own.

Thirst

She counts on the moon
that pours pale milk from its pitcher,
unhurried as a serving girl by a Vermeer window,

not the man with the steel guitar
fingerpicking away the time
before he will take off his shoes
and lay his body
down in their cool-sheeted bed,

not their children grown and gone,
mother buried, father
melancholy still.

She snaps leash to collar,
and they step outside.
Only the dog, she thinks, might understand
how it feels
to drink from the moon's crazed cup.

Advice from the Spoon

The best mirrors distort; don't try to be clever.
Respect the knife and the fork, but grovel in front of neither.

A mouth is a cave you will enter and enter;
you are only a worker, never a guest.

Depend on the testimony of others: sugar is sweet
but you will not taste it. Nor will you taste the bitter remedy.

Silver tarnishes, pewter bends, iron rusts:
look to wood for grain shaped by time.

Nest with your fellows. Despise not
those larger or smaller than yourself.

You will make no music on your own.
Curve and turn, scoop and carry.

Your edge scraped against the famine bowl
plays a song sweeter than any other.

Be kind to smooth gums, be they old or young.
Offend not the mouth guarded by many teeth.

For resting, the floor is as suitable as the table or drawer.
Allow the one who holds you to find your balance point.

If you think you were born to be filled,
remember you were born to be emptied.

I Ask the Gladiola Why She Has No Fragrance

Gone, my boot heels
and those black castanets.
Gone the sharp chords.

Gone, the musk of sweat, of dust,
lemon blossoms unloosed
under the flamenco moon.

Look,
these blossoms were my skirts
that snapped in the wind.

Then three letters, three days
and nights of stolen love,
and the knife.

You ask, so I will tell you—
the blade shone like a promise in my hand.
Now I cannot speak

in any way but this: each day
a new wound opens
on my tower of buds,

my dance pinned
to a stiff green stem.

Each petaled fist
pummels the air.

Blue Malibu

in homage to René Magritte

Summer drives up in a blue Malibu.
She and he, he and she;
their spendthrift delve and dive.

Someone plummets; something slides.
How does anything remain whole?
It's always like this in a story or a dream.

You are running and a door flings open
into a room you do not know.
No lock to keep you out.

The funhouse mirror shatters.
You gather the shards:
cobalt, ruby, violet, gold.

Hold them in your palm, an altar;
your breath, a prayer.
This time, this time you'll discern the pattern.

Mended one, you'll mend;
one hand daring the other to mercy.
Slant the needle, draw the thread.
Pierce and stitch, stitch and pierce.

Brancusi's Sculpture

For the blind, the egg
was the shape Brancusi chose,
as often he chose for the sighted.
In this case, one nearly the size
of a human head.

We cannot see what it will become
or what—if anything—it holds.
White marble, lightly streaked with gray,
suggesting the potential of any egg

until it hatches or is abandoned.
Until it is snatched by fox or crow, or
rolls off a penguin's leathery feet
and cracks in sub-zero night.

The sculpture lies behind plexiglas
touched only by unmoving air and, perhaps,
though rarely, by a curator and her staff,
or a graduate student
who has submitted the necessary forms.

I want to lean my cheek against it,
hold its weight, trace the gray streaks
with my fingertips. I want to steal it,
give it to the blind.

There Are Many to Whom One
Cannot Say These Things

All evers end or mend, I found in my journal;
first in wandering cursive, and then
in soldierly print.

No attribution but *Suzi,*
one of my students, I think.
But who owns anything anyway
at the end?

Sometimes driving home,
just before I make the last turn,
I imagine my house

a smoldering wreckage,
all my belongings released
in ash and smoke, and myself

transformed by
the lift and loft,
the terrible height,
the purge.

The Unobserved Life

The unobserved life is so worth living.
—Talk of the Town

Not the house cat this morning,
not the dented pillows at the head of our bed, or
the magenta geranium biding its time on the sill
after lounging all summer out on the deck.

Not yesterday's kettle of buzzards
gilded by late autumn light
or those crows that briefly rose
then settled back to rip and swallow.

Not the geese conferring as they passed
or the maple leaves sashaying to the ground.
Not my husband bent over the curves of his guitar
or our children grown and gone.

Not my father receding
into the haze of forgetting and sleep
and not—I think—my mother
who exists now only in memory.

His eye is on the sparrow
claims an old gospel hymn, but today—
what a relief—not even
that sparrow is watching over me.

To Make Me Happy

It doesn't take much, just a morning with enough sun for hanging laundry—
the shirts shaken like Gerard Manley's foil, then pinned upside down
so only angels won't fall out of the flapping sleeves.
The checkbook's balanced and there's enough caffeine in my system
to give a buzz that might be mistaken for early bees drunk on crocus.
The dogs sleep in their own spots of sun, and the cat
that's been inside all winter has been shooshed out to air.
The peach and the rose are calling for my shears;
the tulips are circumspect. Daffodil spears, brazen with early warmth,
hoist their frosted tips toward cloudless blue.

There's work in my future, but not today.
My love's heading home and his plane's on time.
I've smoothed the sheets after restless solitude,
letting last night's oboe and clarinet riff replay—the one
Wolfgang concocted for the Adagio of his woodwind serenade.
I'm waiting once more to see if the horns will get a chance before the Minuetto.
Miles of brass spiraled in the horn player's lap. Did she forget, just then,
her own fresh grief? I remembered it for her, we all did,
leaning toward the bright music. At the end, we sprang to our feet.
We wanted to wrap the players in our arms and tackle them,
rolling over and over in muddy grass until the hill gave out,
then rest in the balm of exhaustion.

Sadness and grief have crashed in more backyards than I can count,
but I'm thinking small, charting the little cove of the day:
soon, a run in the park, a trip to the self-service car wash,
a bowl of creamy soup and a square of cornbread.
I'll store up joy like a woodchuck storing fat,
fuel for the moment I know will come, though I don't know when,
don't know what will sucker punch like a schoolboy gone mad,
what will sink into my flesh, slow my breath,
panic my heart to mustang rear and bolt.

Right now it's stillness, not motion, that catches my eye:
eight robins posed in the March-brown grass,
spread and waiting like outfielders in a lazy game with no long hitters.
Their white-ringed eyes focus on whatever absence eyes choose
when sound is the sense that matters. Suddenly one hops, or walks,
and each adjusts position, begins to peck and poke in the duff.
One wings to a low limb at the edge of the field,
and the world's in motion once more. Gulls wheel over the lake.
A couple walking an indolent schnauzer advances
to assure the end of my musing. The day shifts,
clenches down on lists and obligations.

The birds know: reprieve is brief. Even now,
small creatures are gnawing toward our hapless feet.

Epilogue

Writing Like My Friend David

I'd certainly like to write one of those poems
that feels offhand, just casually muse-full,
like walking in the neighborhood late at night,
glancing up only occasionally, but still noticing a bit,
or one that sets out on a familiar half-mile with the dogs
on a cool Sunday morning while the Puritans
are still inside and green is in charge;
a poem that manages to wind its way onto a path
I'd recognize, though I'd never known it existed.
Did I dream it up or go there as a child?
I'm thinking I'd have to be David himself,
but I'm too frenetic, too proud.
I guess that's my way of extended rebellion,
having grown up, as I did, in a house where
pride was embarrassing, if not downright immoral.
But even with the obstacles, I'd like to write a poem
like his. I never learned stilt-walking
or mapped the wild asparagus. Sometimes
I do stop long enough to watch the morning moon
turn from pearl to milk and let the dogs sniff until
they're the ones who resume our ramble.
Sometimes I do, but usually
I tug and make them run.
I'd like to write a poem that knows
its own name but wears it under its shirt,
raises its hand slowly or maybe not at all
when the teacher calls the roll.
All along, both the teacher and the poem know
it's got some heartbreak on its mind, something
you have to do a lot of silent walking to be ready to say;
though if you hum as you walk
and smoke a cigarette or two,
the poem might start talking under its breath,
might start singing in your ear. You'd have to stop
and cock your head to one side

to find out which words are coming from inside
and which are arriving on the wind
and figure out a way to let them mingle.
I'm probably wrong about David
and his poems, but just in case,
I'm letting this maybe poem take its own stroll.
I'm going to walk just a half-step behind
and slow my breathing.
There's something I want to retrieve,
something I want to hold on to.
I'm thinking of Andy, that old black retriever,
and how his walks with David were
full of pissing and writing, pissing and writing
and writing more.

Acknowledgements

Thank you, thank you to the many who have nourished these poems, some with their unwavering quiet support, others with their insightful responses to the poems when they were not much more than seedlings, others with the beauty and bravery of their own writing.

Among them, the Bucks County poetry community, particularly the "pinker" workshop; my Lawrenceville workshop buddies, and the many poets with whom I've worked through Murphy Writing of Stockton University.

The shape of this book owes much to the discerning advice of Chris Bursk for his first read, to Ethel Rackin for gentle and incisive pruning and ordering, and to Ellen Foos, publisher/editor extraordinaire.

Thanks, once more, to Paul for devotion, encouragement, and patience.

US 1 Worksheets: "Song of Ignorance, Song of Bliss," "The Unobserved Life," "Catechetical"

Schuylkill Valley Journal: "On Being Asked to Write a Poem," "Advice from the Spoon"

Poems for the Writing: Prompts for Poets: "Fibonacci Reverie"

And the Questions Are Enough: "Triptych: January 2009"

More Challenges for the Delusional: "Thirst"

River Heron Review: "Listening to Edith Piaf at Nineteen"

Luray Gross, a storyteller as well as a poet, has published
three previous collections of poetry. She works with
students and audiences of all ages as a Teaching Artist.
She was awarded a Fellowship in Poetry by the New Jersey
State Council on the Arts and named as one of their
Distinguished Teaching Artists. She was the 2002 Poet
Laureate of Bucks County, Pennsylvania, where she lives
with her husband and numerous pets.